J   533746
361.6   9.95
Ken
Kent
The story of the Peace Corps

J   533746
361.6   9.95
Ken
Kent
The story of the Peace Corps

DATE	ISSUED TO

GREAT RIVER REGIONAL LIBRARY

St. Cloud, Minnesota 56301

Peace Corps volunteer J. J. Jones tells children about the
new school he will help build in Togo, Africa.

Cornerstones of Freedom

The Story of
THE
PEACE CORPS

By Zachary Kent

CP CHILDRENS PRESS ®
CHICAGO

Senator John F. Kennedy, the Democratic presidential nominee, launched the idea of the Peace Corps at a rally in San Francisco in 1960.

Library of Congress Cataloging-in-Publication Data

Kent, Zachary.

   The story of the Peace Corps / by Zachary Kent.
     p.   cm. — (Cornerstones of freedom)
   Summary: Examines the history of the American volunteer service whose young members dedicated their talents and skills to helping needy people throughout the Third World.
   ISBN 0-516-04752-3
   1. Peace Corps (U.S.) — Juvenile literature.
[1. Peace Corps (U.S.)]
I. Title. II. Series.
HC60.5.K46 1990
361.6 — dc20
                                     90-2113
                                       CIP
                                       AC

PHOTO CREDITS

AP/Wide World Photos—4, 7, 8 (both photos), 12 (both photos), 16, 19 (margin), 21 (left), 22 (right)

Peace Corps—Cover, 1, 2, 3, 9, 13 (both photos), 14, 15, 17 (both photos), 18 (both photos), 19 (bottom left, bottom right), 21 (right), 22 (left), 23, 24 (both photos), 25 (both photos), 26 (both photos), 27 (both photos), 29 (both photos), 30, 31, 32

Pg 2
Peace Corps volunteer Janet Rich of Hudson, Ohio, works at a mother-child health care clinic in the African country of Niger.

Pg 3
Volunteer Sally B. Favor, a Gallaudet College graduate, teaches deaf children at the special needs school in St. Vincent, West Indies.

More than 25,000 excited people jammed into San Francisco's Cow Palace on November 2, 1960. "We want Kennedy! We want Kennedy!" roared the enthusiastic crowd. It was less than a week before Election Day and these Americans eagerly awaited a chance to see the Democratic candidate for United States president.

Deafening cheers, whistles, and applause echoed through the Cow Palace when John F. Kennedy arrived at last. Vigorously the forty-three-year-old senator from Massachusetts strode across the stage. For decades, fatherly older men had occupied the White House. Many Americans believed Kennedy represented fresh ideas and a healthy new start for the nation.

People listened carefully as the candidate began his speech. "One week from tonight the next president of the United States will be turning to the arduous tasks that lie ahead—selecting a Cabinet and preparing a program for peace." In a ringing voice, Kennedy stressed the need for a stronger free world and an attack on world poverty.

"There is not enough money in all America," he continued, "to relieve the misery of the underdeveloped world. . . . But there is enough know-how and knowledgeable people to help those nations help themselves. I therefore propose . . . a Peace Corps of talented young men and women, willing and able to serve their country. . . ." These volunteers, Kennedy explained, would be "ambassadors of peace . . . and serve the cause of freedom."

The idea of a Peace Corps thrilled the Cow Palace audience. During the next days, Americans everywhere discussed Kennedy's bold proposal. On November 8, 1960, Kennedy won the close election against his Republican opponent—Richard M. Nixon. In 1961, as president, Kennedy carried out his pledge and established the Peace Corps. Immediately, many young and idealistic college graduates volunteered for two years' service. Critics loudly claimed the Peace Corps would accomplish nothing. They jokingly called the volunteers "Kennedy's Kids." Since 1961, however, thousands of Peace Corps volunteers have served in dozens of needy foreign nations. Their experiences and friendships have made the world a better place in which to live.

Volunteer service in foreign lands was not a completely new idea in 1960. Missionaries supported by American churches traveled overseas as early as 1809. While spreading their religious faiths in such places as China and India, they also served as schoolteachers, built hospitals, and labored beside

Candidates taking an examination for acceptance into the Peace Corps in San Francisco, 1961

farmers. After the U.S. victory in the 1898 Spanish-American War, President William McKinley sent fourteen hundred American schoolteachers to the occupied Philippine Islands in the Pacific. These dedicated young volunteers spent two years in jungle villages teaching the Filipinos about democracy. During the following decades, dozens of religious organizations continued to send missionaries abroad. In the tragic aftermath of two world wars, American Protestant, Catholic, and Jewish agencies sent thousands of teachers, doctors, and skilled technicians to nations in need.

By the 1950s, American politicians increasingly recognized the value of volunteer foreign service. Wisconsin Congressman Henry S. Reuss, on a journey through Cambodia, noted the small-scale but great success of four young American volunteers teaching there. In January 1960, Reuss rose from his seat in the House of Representatives and urged the establishment of a United States "Youth Corps." In the Senate, Minnesota Senator Hubert H. Humphrey enthusiastically supported the idea, but called it a "Peace Corps."

A book published in 1958 had already caught the imagination of many U.S. citizens. In their novel *The Ugly American*, authors Eugene Burdick and William J. Lederer described the volunteer service of a crude unattractive engineer named Homer Atkins. Instead of living in the pampered style familiar to many U.S. Embassy employees, Atkins,

the "ugly American," lives in the jungle—building water pumps, digging roads, and constructing bridges. Many readers of *The Ugly American* agreed that more volunteers like Atkins should be working overseas.

Finally, John F. Kennedy challenged Americans to take action. During his 1960 race for president, Kennedy made the Peace Corps one of his campaign issues. "How many of you who are going to be doctors are willing to spend your days in Ghana?" he asked listeners while speaking at the University of Michigan on October 14. "We need young men and women," he told another audience two weeks later, "who will spend some of their years in Latin America, Africa, and Asia in the service of freedom." As one of his plans to get the United States "moving again," the Peace Corps received much popular support.

On November 8, 1960, Americans walked to their polling places. By a slim margin of 119,450 votes, John F. Kennedy defeated Richard Nixon. On Inauguration Day, January 20, 1961, Kennedy took the oath of office on the U.S. Capitol steps in Washington, D.C. Then, turning to the huge crowd, the new president gave his inaugural address. The world's future success would require the help of everyone, Kennedy warned. "And so, my fellow Americans," he challenged, "ask not what your country can do for you; ask what you can do for your country."

As president, Kennedy quickly ordered a special task force to organize a Peace Corps. To head this committee, he appointed his forty-four-year-old brother-in-law, successful lawyer and businessman Sargent Shriver. "I recommend that the Peace Corps should be launched soon," Shriver wrote in his final report to the president, "so that the opportunity to recruit the most qualified people from this year's [college] graduating classes will not be lost."

President Kennedy responded swiftly. With the stroke of a pen on March 1, 1961, he signed Executive Order 10924—one of the first major acts of his presidency. By taking this emergency action, Kennedy immediately established the Peace Corps on a temporary basis. Designed to promote world peace and friendship, the new agency outlined three main goals:

I. To help the people of interested countries meet their needs for trained assistance.

II. To help provide foreigners with a better understanding of Americans.

III. To help provide Americans with a better understanding of the peoples of foreign nations.

"Kennedy has started what is surely one of the most remarkable projects ever undertaken by any nation," declared *The New York Times*. Not everyone supported the Peace Corps, however. Skeptics called the new organization a "Children's Crusade" and "Kennedy's Kiddie Korps." Former President Dwight D. Eisenhower immediately dismissed the Peace Corps as a "juvenile experiment." "If you want to send Peace Corps volunteers to an underdeveloped area," Eisenhower joked, "send them to the moon!"

Named director of the Peace Corps, Sargent Shriver promptly gathered the best staff he could find. "We knew the Peace Corps would have only one chance to work," Shriver explained. With great enthusiasm and energy he flew to Africa and Asia in May 1961. In meetings with government officials in seven underdeveloped Third World countries he described the purposes and hopes of the U.S. Peace

President Kwame Nkrumah of Ghana (left). Indian Prime Minister Jawaharlal Nehru (right)

Corps. "From what you have said, Mr. Shriver, the Peace Corps sounds good," stated President Kwame Nkrumah of the African nation of Ghana. "We are ready to try it, and will invite a small number of teachers." In India, Prime Minister Jawaharlal Nehru remarked, "In matters of the spirit, I am sure young Americans would learn a good deal in this country and it could be an important experience for them. We will be happy to receive a few of them." Through the summer, other nations also requested volunteer teachers, nurses, agriculturists, home economists, engineers, mechanics, plumbers, and electricians.

Sargent Shriver (left) was the first director of the Peace Corps.
President Kennedy (right) signed the Peace Corps Act.

While he hurried with recruitment plans, Director Shriver also stalked the offices of the Capitol. In the Senate, Hubert H. Humphrey had drafted a bill for the Peace Corps Act. To win speedy approval, Shriver personally talked to every congressman he could find. The bill was successfully pushed through Congress, and President Kennedy signed the Peace Corps Act into law on September 22. Officially recognized and funded by Congress, the Peace Corps began its work in earnest.

Peace Corps staff members read the applications of thousands of eager volunteers. Any American citizen over the age of eighteen could apply, but volunteers with college degrees or special skills were most likely to be selected. In exchange for two years' service, volunteers would receive very little pay. But the personal image of President Kennedy attracted many recent college graduates to the Peace Corps. "Here was a man with whom I and all young people could identify," explained volunteer Duncan Yaggy, "a man who suddenly made being an American an exciting idea."

During that summer of 1961, the first volunteers gathered on dozens of college campuses for two to three months of training. Busy classroom schedules included language studies, cultural history, sociology, and economics. In addition, outdoor training programs tried to prepare volunteers for the realistic situations they would face overseas. At fitness camps in Puerto Rico and Hawaii, volunteers endured intense physical training. From dawn to dusk the trainees jogged, ran obstacle courses, and climbed cliffs. Those who completed their fitness training felt ready to face any physical challenge that might confront them.

"We put a good deal of hope in the work that you do," stated President Kennedy as he bid the first trained Peace Corps volunteers farewell at a White House ceremony. On August 30, 1961, an airplane

Peace Corp volunteers undergoing fitness training in New Mexico before going to Brazil

touched down and rolled to a stop at Accra airport in Ghana. Fifty-one Americans stepped out and quietly formed a group. Then they sang the Ghanaian national anthem in "Twi," the local language. That surprising performance showed the Ghanaian people that these American volunteers had a real interest in their nation. Spreading out through the country, the volunteers traveled to their separate assignments. In the village of Dodowa, Tom Livingston of Illinois became the first Peace Corps volunteer in action. On September 12, 1961, he started teaching English to a classroom of excited students.

By June 30, 1962, Peace Corps volunteers were serving in seventeen countries. At the start of their bold adventures, many of these idealistic young Americans experienced "culture shock." A volunteer in the Philippines revealed, "When I arrived here, nothing appealed to my sense of taste—not sights, nor sounds, smells, foods . . . I felt completely cut off from everything I had ever known. . . ." Life in remote villages without running water or indoor

Peace Corp volunteer Ted Ellerkamp, Jr., plants rice seedlings in the Philippines.

Left: Volunteer Dick Kirby (left) talks with a resident of Barcelona, Venezuela, about city planning. Right: Jane Bell teaches at Kabare Girls' School in Africa.

toilets greeted many volunteers. As a Peace Corps teacher in Ethiopia, Richard Lipez recalled, "My first real jolt came when I was led into a hut which was the home of one of my students. A fire was burning in the center of the dirt floor, and smoke drifted up through the grass roof." In Venezuela, volunteer Mary Seberger walked through her assigned village and saw hardship and poverty. "What can I—one person—do in two years that will reduce in any way the problems that I've seen?" she helplessly wrote home.

After taking time to adjust to their strange new surroundings, the Peace Corps volunteers rolled up their sleeves and went to work. In classrooms in

Peace Corps volunteers teaching in Senegal, Africa (left), and helping with rice cultivation in Sri Lanka (right)

Ghana, Africa; Malaya, Southeast Asia; St. Lucia, the West Indies, and elsewhere, volunteer teachers chalked arithmetic problems on blackboards and sang American songs to help teach English. Volunteer surveyors in Tanzania hammered markers in the African jungle and supervised teams of roadbuilders. Peace Corps volunteers taught farming skills in India; dug rice silos in Bolivia, South America; and started fisheries in Togo, Africa.

In many ways the Peace Corps workers realized they were making an important contribution. Nurses Nancy Crawford and Kathy Abitz journeyed high into the Andes Mountains of Peru. "The Indians were very suspicious of us when we first arrived," Crawford later recalled. "They have not trusted white people for centuries, but they became friendly as they saw we could make their sick babies smile and relieve their own suffering."

In each foreign country, Peace Corps activities were supervised by a field leader. Peace Corps evaluators also traveled widely to check on the progress of the volunteers. After visiting Senegal, West Africa, evaluator David Hapgood happily reported, "...the volunteers mix with the people instead of staying aloof; they work with their hands with the Senegalese instead of handing down orders." In Sierra Leone, West Africa, another evaluator walked to school with some volunteer teachers. "Peace Corps, Peace Corps," greeted the delighted children running along behind them.

Above: David Hapgood. Bottom left: A Peace Corps physical therapist helps a young victim of an earthquake in Peru. Bottom right: Volunteer Odi Long (left) directs a construction project in Sierra Leone.

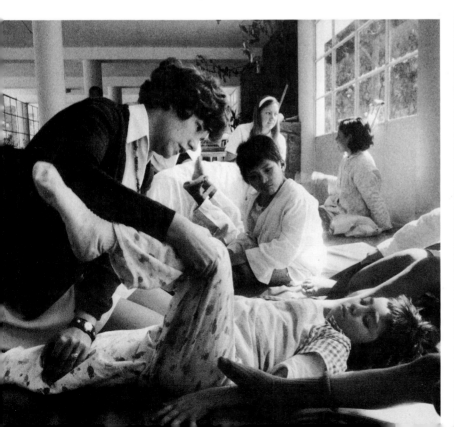

During 1962 and 1963, the Peace Corps continued its good work. Throughout those years, President Kennedy remained closely identified with the organization. "Being in the Peace Corps we all felt we had a special attachment to him," one volunteer remembered. Foreign leaders admired JFK, too. "For the first time," explained President Juan Bosch of the Dominican Republic in the West Indies, "we found in the United States a man who felt as we did, who suffered with us." The Dominicans fondly called the Peace Corps volunteers in their country *hijos de Kennedy*—"Kennedy's children." Thousands of miles away in East Africa, the people of Tanzania called their volunteers *Wakina Kennedy*—"followers of Kennedy." In the remote village of Bassari in Togo, the people named their lone volunteer "Kennedy in Bassari."

On November 22, 1963, in Dallas, Texas, President Kennedy was shot and killed by Lee Harvey Oswald. People throughout the world mourned Kennedy's tragic death. Peace Corps volunteers especially felt a personal loss. Volunteer Maureen Carroll expressed the thoughts of many. "I am proud to have been a part of an already-established living memorial to Kennedy: the Peace Corps."

Through the rest of the 1960s, the Peace Corps matured and prospered. The directors who followed

Sargent Shriver after 1966 gradually changed the
Peace Corps in several ways. The ranks of overseas
volunteers rose to a peak 15,550 in 1966. At the same
time, Peace Corps recruitment more often stressed
the real difficulties of service. "This is how the
Peace Corps measures success," announced a poster
picturing one inch on a ruler. In the midst of the
Vietnam War, many Third World countries resented
U.S. involvement in Vietnam. But anger at the
United States seldom affected respect for the Peace
Corps. A Peace Corps volunteer watched a young
man paint "Yankee Go Home" across a wall in the
Dominican Republic. "Well, I guess that means me.
I'll get packed," remarked the volunteer. "Oh, no!"
exclaimed the Dominican, "I meant the Yankees, not
the Peace Corps."

Left: Peace
Corps Director
Joseph H.
Blatchford
(center) visits
volunteer Tom
Huxtable at a
farm in Kenya.
Right:
Volunteer Bob
Loew works
in Peru.

Left: Volunteer art teacher Barbara Tetrault sketches a rooster for a first-grade class in Ecuador, South America. Right: Larry Sandoval, serving in Ecuador, demonstrates sheep care.

Between 1971 and 1981, the Peace Corps was part of a federal agency called ACTION, before winning total independence again. Those years saw the Peace Corps shrink in size. Training improved, however, as recruits received more intense language study. The Peace Corps also accepted more older volunteers with special skills in forestry, agriculture, health, and engineering. "The Peace Corps—The Toughest Job You'll Ever Love," exclaimed recruitment advertisements in the 1980s.

Through the years, many critics have questioned the success of the Peace Corps. "The economists ask, 'Does it really make a difference what a handful of Peace Corps volunteers accomplish in a small forgotten village of the Andes?'" remarked Director Jack Vaughn. "Yes," Vaughn went on, "it makes a difference to that village."

"Give a man a fish and he can eat for a day," proclaims one Peace Corps slogan, "but teach him to fish and he'll eat the rest of his life." To fulfill its first goal to help people meet their needs, the Peace Corps teaches people how to help themselves. The Peace Corps has had its greatest impact in the field of education. In the 1960s, Nigeria's Minister of Education Alhaji Waziri Ibrahim loudly praised the work of volunteer teachers in that African country: "They have organized libraries. They have given radio lessons. They have created science laboratories. They have produced plays. They have brought a new dimension to physical education in our land." In Africa alone, during the first twenty-five years of the Peace Corps, 25,000 volunteers have taught more than 5 million students. Today, in some fifty

Volunteer George Seay organized a vegetable garden project for boys in a village in Brazil, South America.

Volunteers in South America work on fish farming in Colombia (left) and gardening in Ecuador.

countries worldwide, Peace Corps teachers still meet important educational needs.

Peace Corps volunteers have assisted greatly in agriculture and food production, too. Volunteers have taught the care and management of domestic animals and established fish-breeding farms. They have also introduced new seeds and fertilizers. In Honduras, Central America, for example, volunteer Bruce Burton helped farmers find a U.S. market for a new crop—snow peas. In the West Indies country of Jamaica, volunteer Mike Halpern helped a small group of farmers conduct a market survey. Switching their crop to zucchini squash, these farmers sold 65,000 pounds of zucchini during their first year.

The number of Peace Corps volunteers involved in

forestry rose in the 1980s. The common practice of cutting down and burning forests to provide new farmlands and fuel has threatened to upset the balance of nature in some Third World countries. Peace Corps foresters introduced tree-planting programs to prevent flooding, soil erosion, and air pollution.

Halfway across the world, Peace Corps volunteer Paula Enyeart, a registered nurse, hiked through the mountains of Ecuador, South America. For two years in the 1980s, Enyeart provided the remote village of Cumbijin with its only source of health care. In 1985 alone, Peace Corps nurses, doctors, and health technicians helped over 4 million people in thirty countries. The Peace Corps health programs have achieved astonishing results. They played a

Peace Corps volunteers supervise the construction of a dam and reservoir in Thailand (left) and the planting of tree seedlings in Africa.

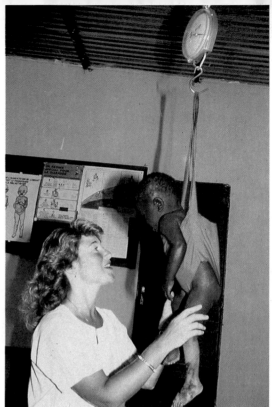

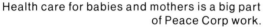
Health care for babies and mothers is a big part of Peace Corp work.

crucial role in eliminating smallpox from Ethiopia in East Africa; tuberculosis from Bolivia in South America and Malawi in Africa; and malaria from Thailand in Southeast Asia.

Overall there can be no doubt that the Peace Corps has fulfilled its first goal—it has surely helped interested countries meet their needs. "Your volunteers work on the real enemies of my people," Guatemala's President Ríos Mont once gratefully explained, "hunger, disease, poverty, and illiteracy."

The work of the Peace Corps has met the requirements of its second stated goal, too—to promote a better understanding of Americans in foreign countries. "The Peace Corps has already erased some

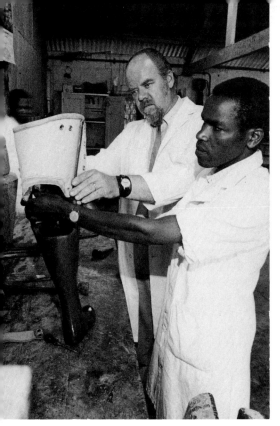
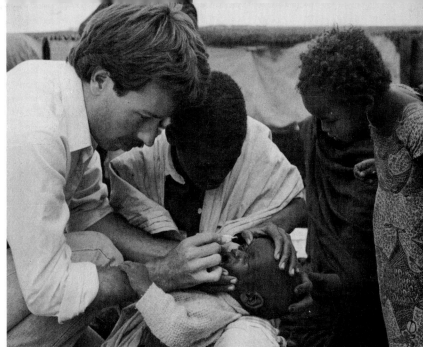

Volunteer Richard Rosenburg (left) shows a technician how to make artificial limbs in Kenya, Africa. Erik Vidstrand (above), working in the African country of Mauritania, treats a child for an eye disease.

stereotyped images of America," President Kennedy told Congress in 1963, "and brought hundreds of thousands of people into contact with the first Americans they have ever known personally." In most cases the volunteers become part of their foreign communities. "We aren't tourists," declared one Peace Corps worker. "I live here. They ask me about what my family life is like, what kind of work I do, the kind of life I have in the States." The bonds of understanding and friendship grow strong and true. Volunteer Jody Olsen, who went back to Tunisia after an absence of twelve years marveled, "...the family I lived with embraced me as if we had never been separated." At the end of two years' service as a teacher in Niger, Africa, volunteer Bertha Evosevich announced to her class that she would soon be returning home to Pittsburgh. "Madame, you can't do that . . ." cried one little girl, "we love you so much."

"Come back and educate us," President Kennedy told a group of departing volunteers in 1961. Since 1961, over 130,000 Peace Corps volunteers have sampled life in 94 different countries. "We are sons and daughters of America," explained veteran volunteer Roger Landrum, "but we are in a sense also sons and daughters of a thousand towns and villages scattered around the world." In fulfillment of its third goal, Peace Corps volunteers return home brimming with valuable experiences.

Most Peace Corps veterans feel a greater appreciation for the boundless wonders found in the United States. Fine schools, jobs, cars, and televisions are unheard of in many foreign places. Volunteers who have served in drought-stricken Africa never again take America's vast natural resources for granted. "I came back to my hometown in Tennessee," recalled one volunteer, "and was livid when I saw a friend of mine washing her car with a garden hose. I remembered my little garden in Niger—how it would have loved to soak up all that water!"

Villager (left) carries a box containing eucalyptus tree seedlings for planting in Niger, Africa. Children (above) learn to read in Haiti, West Indies.

Back in the United States, Peace Corps volunteers put their experiences to good use. With knowledge of some 200 languages and improved teaching skills, thousands work as educators. Others are involved in international work: banking, business, education, and charity. Nearly 40 per cent of the employees of CARE—a private foreign aid group—are Peace Corps veterans. The U.S. government also benefits from the talents of returned volunteers. Many State Department diplomats once served in the Peace Corps. Several members of Congress also draw upon their Peace Corps experiences to help form U.S. international policy.

September 22, 1986, marked the 25th anniversary of the signing of the Peace Corps Act. On that balmy day, 7,000 Peace Corps veterans, staff members, and friends marched through Washington, D.C. At Arlington National Cemetery, they respectfully watched the laying of a wreath on John F. Kennedy's grave. Old and young, white and black, most agreed the Peace Corps had come a long way since the days when volunteers were called "Kennedy's Kids." Today, the remarkable Peace Corps heritage of dedication and courage still inspires volunteers. "The Peace Corps is a vibrant, vital part of U.S. foreign policy," proclaimed Director Paul Coverdell in 1990. As the organization races toward the twenty-first century, over 6,000 active volunteers work

in some seventy countries around the world.
Advanced Peace Corps assistance is helping small
businesses spring up in many Third World nations.
New European programs send English teachers to
Hungary and Poland. In some American schools,
children learn about the world by writing letters to
pen pals in the Peace Corps.

Peace Corps volunteers serve their country and
themselves in mountain villages, steamy jungles,
and across shifting desert sands. "I cannot think of
any group of people who have given more, or given
more generously, than the volunteers of the Peace
Corps...." President Ronald Reagan declared. "In a
troubled world, the Peace Corps is waging
peace.... Growing, learning, and sharing.... Our
volunteers make us proud to be Americans."

Peace Corp Director Paul Coverdell visits a volunteer and friends in the field.

Raising food in the African country of Mali

INDEX

About the Author

   Zachary Kent grew up in Little Falls, New Jersey, and received an English degree from St. Lawrence University. Following college he worked at a New York City literary agency for two years and then launched his writing career. To support himself while writing, he has worked as a taxi driver, a shipping clerk, and a house painter. Mr. Kent has had a lifelong interest in American history. Studying the U.S. presidents was his childhood hobby. His collection of presidential items includes books, pictures, and games, as well as several autographed letters.